The Ancient Maya

JACKIE MALOY

Children's Press®
An Imprint of Scholastic Inc.
New York   Toronto   London   Auckland   Sydney
Mexico City   New Delhi   Hong Kong
Danbury, Connecticut

Content Consultants
Dr. Jeremy Sabloff
Christopher H. Browne Distinguished Professor of Anthropology
Department of Anthropology
University of Pennyslvania

Library of Congress Cataloging-in-Publication Data

Maloy, Jackie.
   The Ancient Maya / by Jackie Maloy.
      p. cm.—(A true book)
   Includes index.
      ISBN-13: 978-0-531-25229-1 (lib. bdg.)   978-0-531-24110-3 (pbk.)
      ISBN-10: 0-531-25229-9 (lib. bdg.)   0-531-24110-6 (pbk.)

1. Mayas—Juvenile literature. 2. Mayas—Social life and
customs—Juvenile literature. 3. Civilization, Ancient—Juvenile
literature. 4. Mexico—Civilization—Juvenile literature. 5. Central
America—Civilization—Juvenile literature. I. Title. II. Series.

F1435.M355 2009
972'.01—dc22   2008053624

1 2 3 4 5 6 7 8 9 10 R 19 18 17 16 15 14 13 12 11 10   62

Find the Truth!

Everything you are about to read is true *except* for one of the sentences on this page.

Which one is **TRUE**?

T or F The ancient Maya were not good farmers.

T or F The ancient Maya thought that crossed eyes were attractive.

Find the answers in this book.

Jade mask from the tomb of King Pakal

Contents

THE BIG TRUTH!

**Corn was a very
important crop for
the ancient Maya.**

El Castillo

Chichén Itzá

The ancient Maya had some of the largest cities in the world in their time.

This figure is made of a green stone called jade. Jade was very valuable to the ancient Maya.

Ancient pyramids like these in Palenque (pah-LEN-kay), Mexico, can be found throughout the Maya world.

CHAPTER 1

The Ancient Maya World

More than 2,300 years ago, the ancient Maya (MAH-yah) lived in the jungles of what is now southern Mexico and Central America. The ancient Maya were ahead of their time in writing, art, and science. They also built temples, pyramids, and palaces. But even with all of their successes, the ancient Maya's **civilization** (si-ve-li-ZAY-shen) ended about 500 years ago.

It took thousands of ancient Maya workers to build a pyramid.

Living and Learning

The ancient Maya lived in Mesoamerica (mez-oh-uh-MER-i-kuh) which includes what are now parts of the countries of Mexico, Guatemala, Belize, Honduras, and El Salvador. Mesoamerica is made up of rain forests, mountains, and coasts. The mountain regions are known as the highlands. Regions that are near sea level are known as the lowlands. From about 250–900 C.E., the ancient Maya had many large cities in the southern lowlands.

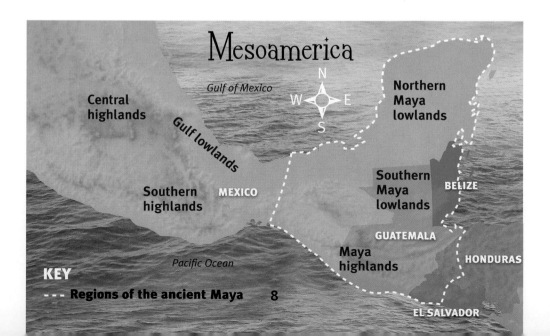

Mesoamerica

Central highlands

Gulf of Mexico

Northern Maya lowlands

Gulf lowlands

Southern highlands

MEXICO

Southern Maya lowlands

BELIZE

GUATEMALA

HONDURAS

Maya highlands

Pacific Ocean

EL SALVADOR

KEY

- - - **Regions of the ancient Maya**   8

Ancient Maya hieroglyphics

The ancient Maya
learned from people,
like the Olmec (OL-mek),
who had lived in
Mesoamerica hundreds of years before them.
Some experts believe that the ancient Maya
created a form of **hieroglyphics** (hi-re-GLIF-ix), or
picture writing, and a calendar by building on what
the Olmec had done. Others believe the ancient
Maya created these themselves.

Thousands of
Maya still live in
Mesoamerica today.

9

Farmers in Guatemala still build houses and clear forests for farming just like the ancient Maya did.

CHAPTER 2

From Farms to Cities

The ancient Maya were excellent farmers. By about 1000 B.C.E., they had learned how to clear the thick brush in the rain forest to grow their own crops. The ancient Maya cut down trees and plants and burned the dead growth. The ash from these fires gave the soil **nutrients** so corn, squash, and other crops could be grown.

Some of the ancient Maya's farming methods are still used by the Maya people today.

Cities of the Rain Forest

Where water was hard to find, the ancient Maya built reservoirs to store rainwater for drinking. They even found ways to make swamps useful for farming. Once the ancient Maya became such skilled farmers, groups of people were able to settle in villages which sometimes grew into cities and **city-states**.

By about 300 B.C.E., the ancient Maya had formed nearly 50 cities in the lowlands of what is now Guatemala. There was no single ancient Maya city that ruled over all of Mesoamerica. The ancient Maya in these different cities were connected by their beliefs in the same religion, myths, and calendar. They were also linked by trade along rivers and paved routes.

This water-filled sinkhole is located near Valladolid, Mexico. The ancient Maya used sinkholes as well as reservoirs for drinking water.

13

This is what one of the temples in Tikal looked like long ago.

Today, all of the temples at Tikal have been restored.

Tikal

Tikal (tee-KAHL) was one of the greatest ancient Maya city-states. It was located in what is now northern Guatemala. At one time, as many as 60,000 people lived there. Some experts believe that Tikal controlled some smaller city-states. However, it never held complete control. Another great city-state, Calakmul (kah-lahk-MOOL), fought with Tikal for power in the region.

Dig This!

Hundreds of years after the ancient Maya left Tikal, people told stories of a great city in the jungle. In 1956, the University of Pennsylvania began an **archaeological** (ahr-kee-oh-LOJ-uh-kuhl) dig in Tikal. They cleared 10 square miles (16 square kilometers) of jungle to uncover ancient buildings. The dig led to many amazing finds, including over 3,000 structures such as temples and palaces. The archaeologists also discovered stelae (STEE-lee) or large slabs of stone on which the ancient Maya had recorded important events.

Scientists have found 70 stelae like this one, that tell the story of Tikal's rulers.

15

Palenque was also known as the "Red City" because all of its buildings were painted red at one time.

Palenque

In what is now Chiapas, Mexico, the ancient Maya built a beautiful city which Spanish explorers named Palenque. The ancient Maya called it *Lakam Ha*, "Big Water," because of its many streams. During its peak between 500–700 C.E., several thousand people lived there. In those years, many hieroglyphics were carved. The hieroglyphics that survived after the city was abandoned have helped experts learn about the city's history and its rulers.

The most famous Palenque ruler was Pakal (pah-KAHL), who became king when he was just 12 years old. He ruled from 615–683 C.E. and is buried in Palenque's Temple of the Inscriptions. Pakal and his son had workers build many of the temples, pyramids, and palaces that still stand today.

Yet, only about a hundred years after Pakal died, the ancient Maya left Palenque. This may have been a result of losing a battle against a neighboring city-state.

This jade mask was found in the tomb of Pakal the Great.

In Maya society, the more important somebody was considered to be, the bigger headdress he wore.

CHAPTER 3

Ancient Maya Society

Ancient Maya **society** had different levels. At the top was the king, his family, lesser leaders, and other important people. At the next level were craftspeople and merchants. Below them were farmers. Slaves were at the lowest level. People worshipped their kings, believing they had special godlike powers.

While the poor wore simple cotton clothing, Maya rulers wore jaguar skins and huge feather headdresses.

Palaces, Pyramids, and Wooden Houses

In jungles throughout Mesoamerica, experts have uncovered the remains of palaces and pyramids that have helped them better understand ancient Maya society. Experts believe that the palaces were home to ancient Maya rulers. Pyramids had religious structures on top of them. The ancient Maya believed these high locations brought them closer to heaven. Some of the temples were used as **observatories** (uhb-ZUR-vuh-tor-eez). Observation of the movements of the sun, moon, and stars was very important to the ancient Maya.

This observatory still stands in the city of Chichén Itzá, Mexico.

Today, some Maya still live in houses like the ones the ancient Maya built more than a thousand years ago.

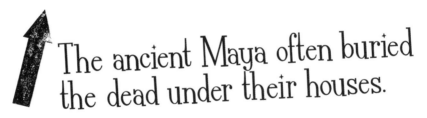

The ancient Maya often buried the dead under their houses.

While the rulers lived in palaces, farmers lived in simple houses with large **thatched** roofs. The ancient Maya built their houses on platforms of dirt or stone to protect them from floods. Though experts have never found one of these houses, they have discovered the platforms that reveal where ancient Maya homes had once been.

El Castillo

The Temple of Kukulcan (koo-kool-CON), or *El Castillo*, is more than 1,000 years old. It is located in the city of Chichén Itzá, Mexico. Experts believe that the ancient Maya constructed the temple to work with their calendar.

At one time, each of the four sides of the pyramid had 91 steps. With the step on the top platform, that made a total of 365 steps—equal to the number of days in a year.

22

To the ancient Maya, Kukulcan meant "Feathered Serpent God."

During the spring and autumn equinox (March 21 and September 22), the Sun lights up one side of the stairway that has a sculpture of a snake head at the bottom of it. It is said that during these events, it looks like the snake is slithering down the stairs.

A wall painting from a palace at Bonampak, Mexico, shows wealthy nobles.

CHAPTER 4

Beauty and Beliefs

Like people throughout history, the ancient Maya had a strong sense of what made people look beautiful. Men and women wore their hair long. Married men and women got tattoos. The wealthy ancient Maya wore animal skins and large feather headdresses. They used jade, a precious stone, to make jewelry. They also inserted small pieces of jade into their teeth. Ancient Maya workers wore colorful clothing made of cotton.

The feathers in rulers' headdresses came from the quetzal (KET-zal) bird.

Beautiful Faces

The ancient Maya believed that crossed eyes were a sign of beauty. Parents may have tried to get their babies' eyes to cross by getting them to focus on objects hanging in front of their faces. The ancient Maya also liked large noses; some ancient Maya used clay to make them look bigger! Parents also tied boards to the front and back of their infants' heads to flatten their foreheads.

Ancient Maya sculpture of a priest

A Serious Game

Like other Mesoamerican people, the ancient Maya played a ball game that had religious meaning. Experts believe that through the game, the ancient Maya acted out battles between gods in both the sky and the underworld. Two teams played against each other in a large ball court with sloped sides. Using their hips, knees, and elbows, each team tried to keep a rubber ball in the air and pass it through stone hoops. Players could not use their hands or feet. Many experts believe that losing teams were sometimes killed and offered as gifts to the gods.

This ball court was discovered in ancient Maya ruins in Kohunlich, Mexico.

Stone hoop

photoHura*

The ancient Maya believed they must pay their gods with blood to be rewarded with good fortune.

Religion

Gods were very important to the ancient Maya. The ancient Maya worshiped gods of nature. Crops, animals, and even people were offered by the ancient Maya to their many gods. Since maize was the ancient Maya's major crop, the maize god was very respected. The ancient Maya believed that this god had the power to help or hurt their farming. When ancient Maya warriors captured enemies, they brought them home as prisoners. In special ceremonies, the prisoners might be killed as offerings to the gods.

Cave Journeys

The ancient Maya believed that after they died, their souls traveled through routes in caves to the underworld, an imaginary world beneath the earth where the dead and spirits live. Therefore, the ancient Maya sometimes buried their dead in caves. They also used caves as places to worship their gods. The ancient Maya thought that their **ancestors** (AN-ses-ters) lived in the caves with the gods of the underworld. These gods, called the "Lords of Death," were imagined to look like jaguars.

Recently, experts have found pathways linking underground caves in Mexico. The caves contained human bones and a temple. These discoveries prove that the ancient Maya sometimes buried their dead in caves.

Some Maya glyphs are pictures of a word.
Others stand for sounds or syllables.
This stela is in Copan, Honduras.

CHAPTER 5

Works of Wonder

Experts have learned about the ancient Maya from the hieroglyphics, buildings, and art that still survive today. The ancient Maya used hieroglyphics, or simple pictures that represent words or sounds. Mostly ancient Maya royalty could write and read glyphs. The ancient Maya carved glyphs into stone and wrote on strips of bark paper, which they used to make books.

The ancient Maya used hundreds of symbols or glyphs.

Sky Watchers

The ancient Maya were skilled **astronomers** (uh-STRON-uh-murz). They watched the sky and noted how the sun, planets, and stars moved. The ancient Maya used their observations to create several calendars that had different purposes. For their religion, they used a calendar with 260 days. For farming, they used a calendar with 365 days, like the one the world still uses today. They also used a Long Count calendar to keep track of longer time spans.

This is a 365-day calendar used by the ancient Maya.

Number Signs

The ancient Maya used just a few symbols for numbers. They based their number system on 20 and were among the first people in the world to use the number zero. With their symbols, the ancient Maya could add and subtract everyday objects. They could also record dates on a calendar. The ancient Maya kept track of their history and culture by carving important dates on stelae.

Works of Art

The ancient Maya created statues, murals, pottery, and carvings. Their art is some of the most beautiful work by people of the ancient world. Sculptors often carved pictures on the flat surfaces of large stones using tools made of **obsidian** (uhb-SID-ee-uhn) or flint, a hard stone. They had no metal tools to work with. Ancient Maya artists painted murals on palace walls. These murals told stories about the Maya's gods and the lives of their rulers.

This sculpture of a Maya sun god is made of stucco, a type of plaster.

34

Ancient Maya artists also created wood sculptures, and painted and wove materials to use as wall hangings. These sculptures and wall hangings decorated the rulers' homes, but did not survive for long in the jungle.

The ancient Maya made beautiful bowls and vases out of clay. The wealthy buried their dead with some of these pieces. The artworks were offered as gifts for the gods of the underworld so that loved ones would be treated well.

Tonina, in what is now Mexico, was one of the last southern Maya cities to exist.

CHAPTER 6

Abandoned Cities

By 900 C. E., the ancient Maya had abandoned the great southern lowland cities. Experts have different beliefs about why this happened. At first experts thought that one single event, like an earthquake or volcano eruption, might have been the reason. Experts now believe that the ancient Maya abandoned their cities more gradually, over about a 150-year span, and that many things contributed to the cities' failures.

After the ancient Maya left their cities, the rain forest grew over the buildings.

Why Did the Maya Leave?

Some experts believe that when cities grew large, they used up too much farmland. Farmers could not grow enough food for all of the people. Other experts think that the rulers' building projects took farmers away from their fields for too long. Scientists now know that a **drought** (DROWT) happened in parts of Mesoamerica from about 800 to 1000 C. E. The lack of water for crops could have hurt farming as well.

Maize made up three quarters of the ancient Maya diet.

The ancient Maya maize god

38

The ancient city of Cancuen (can-QWEN) was located in what is now northern Guatemala. After finding weapons and abandoned palaces there, archaeologists believe that invaders killed royalty and destroyed the city in about 800 C.E.

Some experts think that outside groups or city-states invaded the great cities. Still some others believe there wasn't enough food to keep such large cities running. Many experts do agree that when the cities began to fail, the ancient Maya stopped believing that their rulers had special powers. This made it much harder for the rulers to maintain order and keep the cities growing. Building projects stopped and wars between city-states took more lives. Many ancient Maya died in battle or simply moved away.

The Yucatán Peninsula

After 800 C. E., the Maya continued to live in the northern part of the Yucatán Peninsula. For 700 years, until Spanish explorers arrived, the cities in Yucatán did well. However, these cities were not as large as the earlier southern ones, nor did they have the great art and buildings that the earlier cities had.

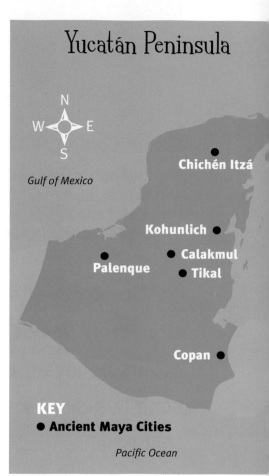

Yucatán Peninsula

N
W E
S

Gulf of Mexico

Chichén Itzá

Kohunlich

Calakmul

Palenque

Tikal

Copan

KEY
● Ancient Maya Cities

Pacific Ocean

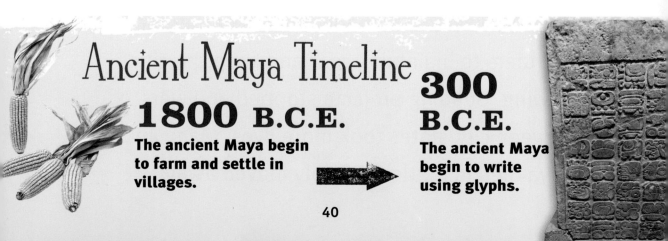

Ancient Maya Timeline

1800 B.C.E.

The ancient Maya begin to farm and settle in villages.

300 B.C.E.

The ancient Maya begin to write using glyphs.

The Spanish Arrive

In 1517, the first Spanish explorers came to the Yucatán. They tried to conquer the ancient Maya, but the Maya fought back. Many of the ancient Maya died in battle. Still more died because they could not fight the diseases that the Spanish brought with them. After almost 170 years, the Spanish finally conquered the ancient Maya. While the ancient Maya people survived, their civilization was destroyed.

Spanish explorers came to Mesoamerica looking for gold.

300 B.C.E.–900 C.E.

The ancient Maya build large cities and become very skilled in writing, math, the arts, and astronomy.

41

1517

Spanish explorers arrive in the Yucatán.

The Maya Today

The Maya continue to live in Mesoamerica today. The largest group is in the Yucatán Peninsula. Just as their ancestors did, these modern Maya grow corn and use some of the same methods of farming. All these years later, millions of Maya still live and work in what was once the land of the ancient Maya. ★

Today, Maya women and girls still dress in traditional woven clothing that their ancestors wore.

True Statistics

Tallest Maya pyramid: Temple IV in Tikal, Guatemala (213 ft. (65 m))

Countries that are part of Mesoamerica: Guatemala, Mexico, Belize, Honduras, and El Salvador

Number of written languages used by the ancient Maya: 1

Number of calendars used by the ancient Maya: 4

Age at which Pakal became a ruler: 12

Number of Maya books on bark paper known to exist today: 4

Largest city during the peak of ancient Maya civilization: Tikal in Guatemala (about 60,000 people)

Did you find the truth?

F The ancient Maya were not good farmers.

T The ancient Maya thought that crossed eyes were attractive.

Resources

Books

Conklin, Wendy. *Mayas, Aztecs, Incas.* New York: Scholastic, 2006.

Coulter, Laurie. *Secrets in Stone: All About Maya Hieroglyphs.* Boston: Little, Brown and Company, 2001.

Coupe, Robert. *Aztecs and Maya.* Sydney: Weldon Owen Publishing, 2008.

Harris, Nathaniel. *Ancient Maya: Archaeology Unlocks the Secrets of the Maya's Past.* Washington, DC: National Geographic, 2008.

Kops, Deborah. *Palenque* (Unearthing Ancient Worlds). Minneapolis: Twenty-First Century Books, 2008.

Mann, Elizabeth. *Tikal: The Center of the Maya World.* New York: Mikaya Press, 2002.

Perl, Lila. *The Ancient Maya* (People of the Ancient World). New York: Franklin Watts, 2005.

Wood, Marion. *Ancient America* (Cultural Atlas for Young People). New York: Facts on File, 2003.

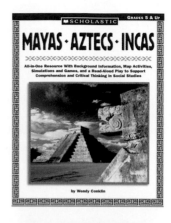

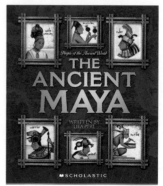

Organizations and Web Sites

Mayan Kids
www.mayankids.com
Visit this Web site for information about the ancient Maya and to play games and do puzzles.

Maya Adventure
www.smm.org/sln/ma
The Science Museum of Minnesota's interactive Web site includes information about the ancient and modern Maya.

Jaguar Sun
www.jaguar-sun.com/mayacities.html
This Web site is packed with research on the Maya.

Places to Visit

National History Museum of Los Angeles County
900 Exposition Boulevard
Los Angeles, CA 90007
(213) 763 3466
www.nhm.org
View the Latin American collection and ancient objects from the Maya world.

University of Pennsylvania Museum of Archaeology and Anthropology
3260 South Street
Philadelphia, PA 19104
(215) 898 4000
www.museum.upenn.edu
The worlds of the ancient Maya and Aztecs have been studied for more than 100 years at this museum.

Important Words

ancestors (AN-ses-ters) – members of your family who lived a long time ago, usually before your grandparents

archaeological (ahr-kee-oh-LOJ-uh-kuhl) – to do with the study of ancient objects and people of the past

astronomers (uh-STRON-uh-murz) – people who study the stars, planets, and space

city-states – states that are ruled over by cities

civilization (si-ve-li-ZAY-shen) – a highly developed and organized society

drought (DROWT) – a long period with little or no rain

hieroglyphics (hi-re-GLIF-ix) – a form of writing made up of pictures and symbols

nutrients – substances that are needed by people, animals, and plants to stay strong and healthy

observatories (uhb-ZUR-vuh-tor-eez) – buildings used for studying the sky and the stars.

obsidian (uhb-SID-ee-uhn) – a hard volcanic glass that can be sharpened

society – the members of a community or group considered together

thatched – having a roof covering made from straw or reeds

Index

Page numbers in **bold** indicate illustrations

About the Author

Jackie Maloy has a bachelor's degree in Theatre from Hamilton College and a master's degree in Communication from University of Nevada, Las Vegas. Her other nonfiction books for children include *Teeth*, *Julia Morgan: Architect*, and *Henry Johnson and Harlem's Own*. After working as an editor at Scholastic Inc. in New York for several years, she moved to Las Vegas, where she lives with her husband and two sons. A few years ago, she and her family were delighted to be able to visit the Maya ruins at Tulum and Coba in Mexico.

PHOTOGRAPHS © 2010: BigStockPhoto (©Daniel Loncarevic, restored temple, p. 14; ©Steve Estvanik, glyphs, p. 40; ©Thomas Pozzo di Borgo, Chickén Itzá, p. 5; ©Walter Zerla, maise, p. 40); Dreamstime (©Paul Hakimata, jade figure, p. 5); Getty Images (p. 3; p. 10; pre-restoration temple, p. 14; p. 17; pp. 28–29; p. 32); iStockphoto (hieroglyphics, p. 9; ©David Parsons, back cover, p. 30; ©Francois Sachs, p. 20; ©Giovanni Rinaldi, pyramid, Uxmal, p. 41; ©Sharon Dominick, p. 4); Photolibrary (cover, p. 6; women, p. 9; p. 13; p. 21; pp. 26–27; p. 38; battle scene, p. 41; p. 42); Tranz (Corbis: pp. 15–16; p. 18; pp. 22–24; pp. 34–36; p. 43; Reuters: p. 39)